How to Write a Best-Selling Book in 30 Days:

An Easy-to-Follow Guide on How To Create, Write and Publish Your Own Book

Written By

David Watson

Contents

Introduction

First off, let me thank you for purchasing *How to Write a Best-Selling_Book in 30 Days: An Easy-to-Follow Guide on How To Create, Write and Publish Your Own Book*, and congratulate you for pursuing either a life-long dream, or a brand new one, in becoming a best selling novelist.

Becoming an author and learning how to be a successful one used to be an "It's not what you know, it's who you know" business, with the prospects of becoming a best-seller. But nowadays, with the technology and general progression from mankind, it is now even easier to follow your dreams, with a multitude of ways to achieve said goals.

Have you dreamed of becoming a best selling novelist? Have you published work before but are looking for more insight? Or, is it just a casual hobby of yours to get better at writing for an audience? Well then, this book is for you!

Did you know, it takes more energy to read a book then it does to write one? Concentrating is more energy consuming than creating. So, using my own knowledge and researching the market, I have put together what I believe are vital points in the transformation to becoming a best selling author. I have squeezed it all into one easy-to-read book, so you can quickly read and teach yourself, whilst not taking too much time, or energy, so you can get straight into becoming that writer you've always wanted to be.

So, without further ado, lets get to it! If you're reading this on a Kindle, or Paperback, I highly advise some note taking throughout, the amount of energy wasted on trying to remember a past phrase or term will only have negative affects, so beat them now by being prepared! Always prepare for success.

Good luck!

Chapter One:
Selecting an Ideal Topic and Title

What Makes a Good Topic for Your Novel?

The topic of your story is the backbone of your novel. You can write with perfect prose and with characters to die for, but your novel might not sell if your topic does not interest the reader. You see, everyone can write a story, but not everyone can be interested in your story. So, the first step in writing your novel is to find a topic that interests people.

Here are some of the things that usually interest readers:

Original Twists

Every reader is a sucker for an original story. But, today, only a few topics can be deemed original. A writer, from the past decade or era, had already written about most of the topics. The question now is, how original is original?

In romance novels, the "Cinderella plot" had been used for over a hundred times, but some novels with the same plot would rise to the top. Some may say that the plot is loved by almost everyone, but many people are easily tired of it. So, what made novels, like "Overnight Cinderella" and "Cinderella for a night" interesting enough that they became best sellers.

The answer is the original twist. The stories in these novels are the same as the fairy tale. They are poor-girl-rich-man stories, but the women in these stories were not the typical Cinderella, who only waited for her prince charming. They were Cinderella's, who ran after their reluctant princes charming. Among hundreds of "Cinderella plots", having some of these twists could set your novel apart.

Another example is Stephenie Meyer's "Twilight". Many vampire or Dracula plot stories had a vampire with a love interest. However, in most of these stories, the woman becomes afraid when she finds out that the hero is a vampire or she does not end up with the vampire.

In "Twilight", you have a teenager, who is very much in love with the vampire and wants to be a vampire herself, and a vampire, who refuses to make the heroine into a vampire. This simple original twist became a cultural phenomenon.

It is always good to write an original yourself, but if you are not gifted with originality, go for an original twist. So, how do you do it? Here are some ways:

1. *Change the genre of a classic plot.*

Take the "Cinderella plot". It is always used in romance novels. Turn it into a crime mystery. You have a Cinderella character, who is also a sleuth and a prince charming, who is also the murderer. You retain that romance between them, but you would have to tear them apart because of the conflict between them. The conflict between the characters may be enough to make your novel stand out.

2. *Create a second lead out of a less significant character.*

A good example of this is the genie character in Disney's Aladdin. In the original story of Aladdin, the genie was not really a significant or a lovable character. But, when Disney portrayed it into a lovable character and incorporated it to the characters of the hero and the heroine, the story became more interesting to a certain market.

3. *Change the setting.*

A setting can turn a typical plot into a new story. If you take the "Cinderella plot" and put in a dystopian setting, the other readers may forget about the ordinary plot and think that it is something different.

Characters

There are novels, which the ideas are the characters itself. Take the Harry Potter novels. Do you think it would have become a best seller if the story was about Hogwarts and not Harry Potter? It probably would not because it was Harry Potter, and other vital characters, who brought life to Hogwarts.

There are three types of characters that can keep your idea interesting.

1. *A Character who is the idea of the journey*

This is also known as the "hero journey plot". The idea is the struggle of the character while he is on a journey. An example of this is the Odyssey. The poem tells the journey of Odysseus, as he returns home. Without the character of Odysseus, there would be no story.

Harry Potter can also be viewed to be this type of character. Other characters are brought to life because of his characters and these other characters only joined him in his journey.

2. *A character that is the "Spirit" of the story*

This character is essential in the novel. Without such character or characters, the story would not develop. They are often called the "hook" characters. They are the characters that will draw your reader to the story.

A good example of this type of story is the "Lovely Bones". The story is about a family, which was devastated by a murder, but the introduction of Susie Salmon as the storyteller made her the spirit of the story. If Susie Salmon only remained as the victim, the story would still develop. But, with the addition of her character, the novel became more interesting. Her spirit added a twist on the story.

3. *A character who adds conflict or gives light to the conflict*

In many novels, this character exists. The character is known as the "Pandora's box" character. His entry or death will create the conflict to the hero. The character may not be the lead character, but his character is where the hero derives his character.

An example of this is Sophie Neveu Saint-Clair of the Da Vinci Code. She is not the most significant character in the novel, but she sheds light to a question or conflict in the story, without which, the story will not be complete.

Market and Trend

Another way to develop a good idea for your novel and keep your readers interested is the market and the trend. If you want to be a best seller, your book should be in a right market.

There are many books which are worth reading, but they do not make it to the best seller's list. One of the main reasons is that it did not fit the market and the current trend.

If you tried to publish a novel about a girl falling in love with an angel, at the time the vampire romances were a hit, your book might be overshadowed by these novels. Even if your characters and your ideas are a thousand times better than the "vampire" plot, some of the readers might not take a look at your character, because they would be out of the trend.

Making your novel fit the market and the trend can be difficult. You may get many criticisms if you publish a book with almost the same plot and characters as the book that started it all. However, you can always make your story speak for itself. This is what is called as "pitching".

Pitching, in fiction writing, is deducing your plot into less than 50 words. This can be your novel's blurb in the future. If you manage to create a pitch that is different than the rest, your novel might climb up the best-seller ladder.

Here are some characteristics of a good pitch:

1. *It tells the story, but not the end.*

After you thought of an idea that is within the purview of the market, write a good pitch that tells your story, but not the ending. If you manage to do this and your pitch is different from the rest, you probably have a good idea.

For example, you want to write a Harry Potter type of story. Write first a pitch about Harry Potter. Let's assume this pitch:

> "Harry Potter is a wizard boy who survived an evil revolution and is tasked to stop the resurgence of another evil revolution."

Basically, the pitch would tell you that someone attacked Harry Potter, but somehow, he survived and he is now fighting evil. This pitch might be enough to intrigue the readers. How did he survive the attack? What evil? How can he defeat evil?

Now, if you want to write a story similar to Harry Potter, you have to write a pitch that is almost the same, but different. For example, you can write:

> "A young wizard was saved from an evil invasion and underwent training to fight the evil ruler and get his town back."

Here, it is obvious that the story is somehow the same, but your story is about surviving an evil invasion and getting back at the ruler. The questions would still be the same. How did he survive the attack? What evil? How can he defeat evil? But, now, the evil pertains to a different premise.

2. *It tells the obvious plot, but does not make it too obvious.*

> "A poor girl falls in love with a rich man and they lived happily ever after."

If you write the pitch above, do you think anyone would be thrilled to buy your book? The readers might not. The plot is too obvious. It is another Cinderella story. However, if you write it like this:

"She can't have him. He wants her. But, money gets in the way."

Here, the plot might be obvious. A girl and a boy meet. There is a romance brewing, but something hinders them. What could it be? How will they meet? What will happen if they meet?

When you think that your pitch has a spark, then you can get back to developing your plot, your characters and organizing the flow of your story.

Its by following these easy preparation steps that will induce a creative beginning to the development of your novel, and help cement a bestselling plot/storyline for your very first novel!

Excited yet?

You   should   be.

Chapter Two:
Organizing Your Chapters

Steps in Creating Chapters for Your Novels

The greatest obstacle for every writer is not about developing a topic or an idea. Many writers, even those who had written dozens of best sellers, struggle to start writing. However, many writers also tend to get carried away the moment they start writing. They would write what comes to their mind. It is a good thing, but some writers tend to deviate from their idea and their plot.

So, before you begin to write, try to organize your chapters first. Here are the steps:

1. *Expound your idea or pitch into a full-blown plot or summary.*

Make a short story out of your idea or your pitch. You do not have to include the dialogues first. You just have to write how the story would flow. Your plot should include:

- *The setting or the world.* Roughly describe the setting of your story. You do not have to describe how the actual setting looks like. You could just make a collective description, e.g., Hawaii during World War II, 19th century London.

- *The characters and their identities.* Who are your characters? What should they look like? How should they be introduced? How they would meet?

- *The "hook".* In writing, the hook is the happening or situation that would spark the story or tells the reader the genre of the book. Some thinks that it is the same as conflict, but it is different.

  - For example, a hook is a "murdered person who was found in the dumpster." A conflict could not be about the murdered person, but a corruption in the police force, which was discovered because of the murdered person.

- *The conflict or the problem the characters would have to resolve in your story.* Most of your story would be controlled by the conflict. The harder the conflict, the longer your novel would be. However, the conflict can also give you a hard time. Before you introduce a conflict, make sure that you know how to solve it.

- *The climax.* It is the most exciting part of the story. But, in your plot, it is where you point when the secret or the solution to the conflict would be revealed and the situation that would try to suppress that revelation.

- *The resolution.* Basically, it is how you want your novel to end. Will it end in a happy ending, a tragedy or a compromise? You can end your story in any way you like, provided, that it is directly connected to your conflict.

You cannot write a conflict between Cinderella and her Prince and resolve it with Cinderella discovering who killed her father.

2. *Divide your story or summary into chapters*. Breaking your novel into chapters is not mandatory when writing a novel. However, as a writer, you should think of your readers. Only a few readers could read a book in a sitting. Some of them would only read a few pages or chapter at a moment. It would be helpful on their part if your novel has chapters.

Another reason you need to divide your story into chapters is the pacing of your story. You can slow down and give a suspenseful effect to your story by ending one part and beginning the other in a different view or page.

Also, chaptering is essential if your novel includes shifts in settings or characters. For example, if you have a time travel plot, you may need to write a different era on a separate chapter.

Dividing your story into chapters may vary, but there are certain chapters that are almost fixed. These are the first and the last chapter of your novel.

a. *The first chapter*. This is where you should always introduce the hook, the setting, and some of the main characters. As you approach the end of this chapter, you will have to introduce hints of what the real conflict should be.

b. *The ending chapter*. This chapter may start with the climax and end with the resolution. However, many novels always allot this chapter for the resolution of your novel. Some novelists also treat this chapter as an epilogue.

The middle chapters would talk about the conflict and the hints of finding the solution. These chapters may also include sub-stories or back stories of some characters. Second leads and other characters are often introduced in the middle chapters.

3. *Outline your middle chapters*. The first chapter and the ending chapter are almost definite. Their points are often similar. However, outlining your middle chapters is a different and a more difficult task. A single poor chapter can change the view of the reader about your novel. Thus, it is important that your middle chapters should be exciting and outlined correctly. Here are some important points you should consider when outlining your middle chapters:

- *The point of the chapter*. In every middle chapter, you should always introduce a point or purpose of the chapter. Many novels introduce the conflict in the second chapter. You can use that as the purpose of the chapter. You can put more fuel in your conflict for the next succeeding chapters.

    Make sure that the succeeding chapters would have a point connected to the second and/or previous chapter.

- *Captivating scene or dialogue*. Every middle chapter should be significant, even in a small way. You should think of a captivating scene or a dialogue that must be included in that chapter. These scenes can become the point of reference to your readers. When one of your chapters becomes vague, they might easily remember a situation from a certain chapter that can help them understand.

If your reader is stuck in a certain chapter, they might not continue reading your novel.

- *A cliffhanger.* A good novel puts a reader on the edge of their seat in every end of the chapter. Your chapter should aim to make the reader become excited to discover and resolve your story. It should have a question that has to be answered in the next chapter or an answer to a question from a previous chapter.

  However, as you approach the last parts of the story, your chapters should include more answers than cliffhangers.

4. ***Countercheck your outline with your plot.*** There are times that your outlines or the points in your outline deviates from your original plot. Your novel may not have the same effect as the shorter version. There are instances that your outline becomes better. But, there are also instances where your story is overshadowed by your creativity and description.

Thus, you always have to check your plot when outlining your chapters. Also, do not be contained by your plot or your novel when writing. Always feel free to add more or to reduce something, when you think it would not help your story.

Chapter Three:
Blueprinting Each Chapter

Why Provide a Blueprint for Your Chapter?

Many writers skip this step when writing their novels. They only rely on their chapter outlines when writing their stories. However, an outline does not tell you exactly what would happen in the chapter and how each chapter relates to each other.

Blueprinting your chapters will help you write your first draft more effectively. You will get all the points and the scenes needed in your chapter, so you do not get lost as you write the succeeding ones.

Also, when you have a blueprint, you describe your settings, characters and events better.

Steps in Blueprinting your Chapter

A chapter blueprint is like a movie board, but you do not necessarily have to draw it. All you need is to jot down in your notebook or any piece of paper. Here are the steps on how you can create a blueprint for your chapter:

   1. *Brainstorm.* Before writing your chapter, imagine first what would happen in the chapter as provided for by your chapter outline.

For example, you are writing about a soldier coming home to Okinawa after World War II. In one chapter, you might consider writing about the following:

    a. A soldier returning home to his family. What was he doing to show that he was returning home to his family? Here you can talk about where he was. Was he riding in a car, a train or anything to get home?

    b. He did not recognize his wife and his children. What made you say that he did not recognize his wife and his children? Why couldn't he recognize them? What did he do to his wife? To his children?

    c. His family became worried about him. How can you show that his family was worried about him? What did his wife do? What did his children do?

2. *Sketch your setting.* After you have settled with what you want to write in your chapter, sketch your settings in every scene. You do not have to draw it. You just have to describe it in writing.

For example: When the soldier was returning home, how did Okinawa look like from the train? Describe the structures your character saw. Also, talk about other things that are happening next to him that could show that he was returning home to his town. You can note that:

- The cherry blossoms bloomed beautifully.

- The train was packed with other soldiers.

- The train was noisy and it passed a broken railway.

Then, write about the next scene. Like when the soldier had gone home. You can write about:

- The structure of their house. What was it made of? How big or small it was. Or,

- Describe a significant painting that can show a defining trait of your character.

Continue describing the setting until you could clearly visualize the world through your notes.

3. *Sketch your characters.* When you are developing your idea or your story, you would already have the lead characters in your mind. You may also have a sketch of their appearance, like the color of their hair or their eyes, their height and even their body build.

But, when you are blueprinting your chapter, you do not just stick to your original character sketch. Characters change their appearance according to the scene. That is what you are going to write.

We take the example of the soldier. A few months after the war, his face would undergo changes. He might grow some beard or he might gain some weight. These tiny points can also help your reader imagine your world and understand your story as it progresses.

4. Note down the important dialogues. Dialogues are as important as the narratives. Readers could understand them more than the narratives. They make the scenes more memorable.

As you try to imagine your chapters, some of these dialogues would naturally pop out in your mind. Be quick to jot them down. Raw dialogues often have the best impact. But, if you have difficulty writing a dialogue, try to write it plainly.

Ask yourself how you would respond to the situation or a previous dialogue. You can always add more impact on your dialogue as you write your drafts.

Write anything that each of your character may have to say. Do not leave any dialogues just because you think it is unnecessary, ineffective or a cliché. These dialogues might work with your story as you write.

So, to conclude this chapter, it is just as important to blueprint your chapters, then just to outline them. Remember to explain to your reader everything you can to make the scene they set in their minds as identical to the scene you yourself imagined and wrote.

Chapter Four:
Mindset for Fast Writing and Production

Many aspiring novelists want to finish their novel as fast as they can. There are a lot of factors that will affect this mindset.

One, you do not want another writer writing and publishing a similar idea or topic. Every true novelist wants to be the original. So, the remedy, write and publish your story as soon as possible.

The second reason is the payment or royalty. The earlier your novel is published, the sooner you get your royalty or your payment.

But, even if you have these motives, writing and producing your novel can still be a challenge, especially in this era. You would think that with the technology now, it would be faster to write. For some, it becomes more difficult because there are a lot of things you can do with your computer or laptop. We have distractions everywhere we go. It is difficult for writers to just sit down and write.

So, how do you develop a mindset for faster writing and production? Here are some suggestions:

1. *Be an old school writer*. Write your ideas, blueprint, and even your first draft with pen and paper. A notebook or a piece of paper will not present any distraction, unless you are also into paper crafts or the odd doodle. We all

do it. A pen may not make you write as fast as the keyboard, but it could make you write better, and rawer.

According to a study, when you hold something that fits your work, it becomes an extension of your hand. It follows your mind. So, when you use a pen, it could make the idea slip faster, unlike when you are typing.

Also, when you write by hand, you do not worry that you would hit a wrong key. You do not worry about your spelling or grammar because nothing would correct it at first. Whereas, when you write using your computer, you might get distracted when you hit the wrong key or when a notification line appears under your words.

If you are lazy to write, you can keep your ideas or parts of your novel by recording it with a voice tape recorder. Try not use your smartphones for it. Old school voice recorder could not as easily be deleted. Your recording will not be stopped or distracted by a phone call or any notification. You could just tell your story just as how you would want to write it.

2. Surround yourself with things about your story. You can focus and write faster if all you could think about is your novel. Surround yourself with items that can stimulate your interest towards your idea and help arouse your creativity.

For example, if you are writing a romantic "Cinderella plot" novel, surround yourself with other books with the same story or a picture of your lover. You can also place flowers or anything romantic near you as you write. Play a nice romantic song in the room.

Do not place anything you are interested in, but remotely connected to your story, near you. It can tickle your brain into doing something else. You might end up cooking something or doing another project instead of writing.

3. *Set a schedule.* Many creative writers do not set a fix schedule. They write when they feel like doing it. But, having a schedule will help you finish your novel faster. It will help you set up your writing space, without sacrificing the other things you like or the other people around you.

Even if you are doing it as a hobby or to simply accomplish a dream, treat it as your job, which you have to attend to at a certain hour of the day and you need to focus on.

4. *Assign a deadline for your novel.* Working in schedule can make you write faster, but, it might not let you produce a quality work. It could become just an endless routine for you. So, to help you produce a novel better and faster, you need to assign a publisher.

Just ask a friend to be your publisher. Let them set a submission schedule for your drafts. Knowing that you have a deadline can encourage you to work faster and turn in quality work.

5. *Enjoy your writing time.* Some people, especially those who make a living or those who hope to earn millions with their novels, tend to put pressure on themselves. Writing becomes their life, instead of being an escape from their reality. It becomes a burden, instead of a blessing.

Writing your novel should be fun. It should help you relieve from your stress. It is supposed to take you out of the real world and make you rule the world you created. It should always excite you even if it is a tragedy or a thriller.

More ideas would come to you if you are comfortable. You would love to write more, instead of finishing your novel, just to end it.

6. *Eat and sleep well.* Studies proved that a hungry stomach and/or a sleepy brain produce less work. Hunger affects your creative hormones and sleepiness gives you less energy. No best-selling novelist or classic writer wrote with an empty stomach or when they were sleepy. No one can write with an empty stomach or when they are dead tired.

If you do, you will get sick, become tired easily or die. Then, you would not finish your novel at all. So, remember to eat up and rest up.

If you want to finish your novel fast, eat well and have enough sleep. You could focus and retain more information when your body is not trying to distract your brain.

I can't stress enough about following this chapter almost religiously. If you've read the chapter and thought about easy, corner cutting replacements for some of these tips then I guarantee you'll get nowhere. Writing your own book doesn't have to be hard. Sure it can be difficult at times, but there is no reason you can't be in complete control whilst writing it. Taking theses points seriously will set you on your way to being a bestseller. And, also train you into being the most efficient author you've always wanted to be, and soon you won't need to follow certain steps because you've taught yourself the important habits of being a writer, and can continue to stay consistent

Baby steps, my future writers, baby steps.

Chapter Five:
Your Blunderbuss First Draft

What is "Blunderbuss"?

blun·der·buss

ˈbləndərˌbəs/

noun

1.

an action or way of doing something regarded as lacking in subtlety and precision.

"Instead we got a policy and political blunderbuss who must not have been paying attention during the 2017 presidential campaign"

Creating a "blunderbuss" first draft, means to jot down a first draft with almost no decorum, just be at one with the creativity, and write! No, your blunderbuss draft will not be a bestseller, but it is from here that a raw, authentic story will be created, giving you an adequate foundation to create a bestseller on.

The Crucial First Draft

Only a few aspiring novelists can finish their first draft. The standard novel has an average of about 40,000 words. A writer does not only need creativity to write that long. He also needs patience to do it. Many writers do not have that patience.

Moreover, fewer novelists finish and produce their novel after their first draft. There are many reasons that attributes to this. Here are some:

1. ***The writer becomes frustrated after reading his first draft***. When you read through your first draft, you will find misspelled words, wrong grammar, missing words and awkward sentences. Also, some of the scenes you intended to show might not come out as you once planned.

Many writers get frustrated because of it, especially if the problem is at the first part of the draft. When you change something in the first part, be it the tone, scenes and accuracy, the rest of the novel may be affected. You would end up repeating the whole thing. Some writers would rather abandon the whole novel than rewrite it. Mistake.

2. ***Lack of patience.*** You had kept your patience writing more than 40,000 words. When you find out that you have to change some scenes or delete some parts you have written, you tend to become impatient. This could result to either stubbornness or abandonment. You would either submit your manuscript filled with blunder or you abandon it. Either way, nothing will be published.

3. ***The writer becomes bored of his own novel.*** This usually happens to writers who do not think about their readers. They think of writing as a way of getting their ideas out. They do not think about perfecting their story.

These writers stick only to their idea. They do not care about how the story flows. So, when they proofread or edit their novel, they become bored. They are not focused when they edit because they read with their memory and not by their eyes. When they finished their rash proofreading or editing, they do not care about their novel anymore. They already get a sense of accomplishment. They either submit it with the blunders or keep it to themselves.

The problem, however, when the manuscript is returned because it was lacking in certain areas, these writers tend to become frustrated and completely abandon the novel.

Getting Pass the First Draft

The real challenge of writers is to keep moving after the first draft. If you have few mistakes in your first draft, you are more likely to finish your novel. Thus, it is important to minimize these blunders and distractions, so you can focus on improving your first draft rather than rewriting it. Here are some of the ways to minimize mistakes in your first draft:

1. Be patient with your blueprint. Your blueprint can help you minimize the mistakes of your novels. It will also keep the accuracy of your story as you progress. Make a complete blueprint of each chapter before writing your story. Make sure that you do not forget to include significant scenes or points in your blueprint.

Stick to your blueprint, as much as possible. Remember that it is easier to delete the excess scenes than creating a new one after you have finish your first draft.

2. Refrain from using fancy words in your first draft. Write your scene as it comes to your mind or how you jot it in your blueprint. Simpler words can be changed into fancy words in your second and third drafts. Looking for the right elegant words would just take too much of your time. Don't do a Joey Tribbiani.

The purpose of the first draft is to get your idea on the paper. You are not writing to impress your readers. Just as William Forrester said in the movie Finding Forrester, "Write your first draft with your heart."

3. ***Do not be bothered with your grammar.*** The brain is always faster than the hands or any voluntary muscles in the body. Even if you are a grammar nerd, you are bound to have a slip when you are writing your first draft. You will always get a missing or misspelled word. You will have sentences with wrong punctuations,

As you write your first draft, let go of any grammatical errors you see. Just note the errors you see, but avoid correcting it as you write. You might forget your ideas or what you wanted to write, if you go back and forth correcting your mistakes.

4. ***Do not to do additional research while writing.*** The reason most writers fail to write fast is because they tend to research as they write. They check the accuracy of the basis of their story. They want to make their world as real and as relatable as possible.

Avoid researching while you are writing your first draft. You should do it when you are organizing and creating blueprints for your chapters. Pausing to research something about your novel may not affect your ideas, but it will distract you from finishing your novel faster.

5. ***Proofread or edit part of your first draft only if you ran out of ideas to continue with your story.*** Writers always bump into a wall when they write. They still

have an idea to write, but they become less interested to write. Sometimes, they want to write, but the idea is gone. These moments are a good time to proofread or edit the parts you had written.

Your disinterest or lack of idea would help you become objective when correcting your work. You will not also feel rushed when doing it.

More importantly, as you proofread what you have already written, your refresh your mind and awaken that creative idea that may have been buried or awaken your passion to write again.

You can also do your additional researches when something seems to block your ideas. You can always find something that would crush that writer's block.

The moment you get into the zone of writing again, stop proofreading and get back to writing.

6. *Always bear in mind that your first draft will always be a secret to your reader.* Your readers will only read your finish or published work. At that moment, your work may already be free from any blunders. Your readers may start praising your writing. They will never know anything about your first draft.

Your readers will judge your finished book not your first draft. So, free your mind from any worries and just tell your story as you want it. It's called a draft for a reason. Like the first time you tried to make cupcakes and they grew to the size of softballs, practice makes perfect.

7. _Try writing the beginning and the end chapters first._ Every story has to have a beginning and an end. Many writers find it easy to finish their first draft when they already have written the end. It inspires them to finish their story.

Once you have a beginning and an end, your story is almost finished. You would feel that it would be a waste if you stop writing or abandon your novel. And so would I, please don't give up!

Chapter Six:
Managing Energy for Creative Focus

Improving Your First Draft

Finishing your second and succeeding drafts may not be as challenging as your first draft, but it does not make things easier for you. Your second draft requires you to be more creative, but as a reader and not as a writer.

Readers are as creative as the writer. Many of them have better imagination than the writer. Writers express their imagination well, while readers understand and heighten the writer's imagination.

To improve your first draft, you have to become a creative reader. It is only then that you can understand your story better and see any flaws on how your story flows.

However, having that creative focus is also a challenge. Most of your creativity may have been drained while you were writing your novel. You may not have that energy to retain the focus you need to be a reader. Thus, it is important to manage your energy when you are trying to improve your first draft.

Steps in Managing Your Energy to Improve Creativity Focus

1. Do something that makes you happy. Some studies show that people who are having fun becomes more creative than people who are sad. Happy people have more things to be thankful for and less things to fear. They are thankful for the blessings they have, which make it easier for them to imagine happy or joyful things. They are afraid to lose the things that make them happy, thus they can imagine the sorrow, fear and hatred of losing that happiness.

If you are happy, you are also inspired to do or make something better. You have more energy to draw creative outputs and focus.

2. ***Do not rush when reading your first draft.*** Readers do not read the whole novel in one day. According to some statistics, an avid reader can only keep reading for twenty minutes. A reader would naturally take a break, either to rest or to absorb what he just read. After 10 to 15 minutes of reading, the brain would start to refuse other information that you read. Thus, you would no longer comprehend what you are reading and would become lost.

To help you save your energy and become more creative, take a 10-minute break after a 10 or 15 minute reading time. Do not worry if you are nearing an exciting part. The break will help you think about the next scene and help develop it.

3. ***Focus your energy to one thing at a time.*** Multi-tasking can make you finish more things faster, but it gives you less energy to fuel the creativity in you. If you are reading or trying to improve your first draft, you should focus on that alone. Remove any distraction that can take away your focus from your story.

Like when you are writing your first draft, you should also set a schedule to read it. You should observe the same working environment you had when you were writing your first novel. You could focus and criticize the creativity of your novel if it is the only subject of your concentration.

4. Eat and sleep well. Whether you are writing or reading, you drain energy. The lower your energy, the faster it depletes. Reading is more exhausting than writing. It is always harder to think than to express.

If you are hungry or sleepy, you will not have the energy to think while you are reading. Your first draft is already hard to understand because of the blunder. Reading it while you are hungry would exhaust you faster.

It will be hard for you to appreciate the story or to think something to make the story better. Also, you will read slower, delaying your production more.

5. Exercise. Researches show that people, who exercise daily, often feels euphoric and inspired when working. They have more energy to work and can produce more. The same is true when you are trying to improve your first draft, or even when you are writing your first draft.

However, exercise is more effective when you are trying to improve your first draft. People tend to relax better after an exercise. If you read your first draft while you relax, you become optimistic. It is easier for you to decide whether to retain the scenes you wrote or to improve them.

Also, do not forget to exercise your eyes, too. Fresh eyes can help you read longer. You can review your draft faster.

Strengthen your eyes' near and far focusing.

Sit in a chair or stand in front of a blank wall. Place your thumb about 10 inches in front of your face and focus on it. ...

Then, focus on an object that is 10–20 feet in front of you without moving your head. ...

After 10–15 seconds, refocus on your thumb.

6. ***Avoid correcting your first draft.*** It would be difficult to focus your energy into creativity if you are also focusing on the writing technique, grammar and spelling of your first draft. Save the correction after you finished improving your first draft.

To help you manage your creative focus until you finish your novel, you may keep these suggestions in mind.

    a. Write your first draft with your heart and mind as a writer.

    b. Improve your first draft with the mindset of a reader.

    c. Write your second draft with a mindset of a teacher. It is only then that you could focus on the technicalities of your novel.

Chapter Seven:
Creating a Cover of Your Book

The Challenge of Creating a Book Cover

Creating a cover would not be a problem if your novel is going to be published by a publishing house. Your publisher would take care of the cover of your book. But, if you intend to publish your book through Kindle publishing or any individual publishing, you need to think about your book cover.

"Do not judge the book by its cover."

You may have heard it a lot of times. Sadly, most readers judge the book by its cover. The color, the illustration, and the implication of the cover can influence the interest of your reader. That is how important it is.

Creating a cover is almost as complicated as developing an idea. Here are some points that you should think about when you are creating your cover.

1. ***Your cover should tell your readers a chunk of what your story is about***. Do you think people would have bought the Harry Potter books if the cover was plain black with a broom? I don't think so. The cover does not tell anything about the story.

Your cover should show what your novel is about. A romantic novel could have a book cover where two people hold hands or kiss. A cover with an illustration of a dead body can convey to the buyer that it is a crime novel. Do not make your reader guess what your novel is about.

There are exceptions to this rule. However, you have to be a recognized writer first before you can bend this rule. Famous writers may care less about the cover because their name could already attract the readers.

2. *Less is more.* Your cover may need to tell part of your story, but you do not have to fill up your cover with illustrations. You should know how to balance the idea of your story, the effects of your cover, the title and of course, your name.

As an aspiring novelist, apart from telling what your novel is about in your cover, you are also telling the reader who you are.

One good way of highlighting your name is to create a significant white space between your illustration and your name. Also, avoid placing your name below the title, especially when you are trying to make people remember your name.

3. *Follow the trend in the market.* Making your book cover is like creating the topic of your novel. It has to follow the trend for the specific genre. If a certain genre, like romance novel, use caricature or silhouette illustration for the cover, you should try to follow that trend.

However, be careful about intellectual property rights. If you copy the idea too much, you might get in trouble for infringement. Just follow the concept, but not the whole cover.

4. *Do not forget the back cover.* If you are only publishing an e-book, a back cover may not be as important. But, if you plan to also publish it in paperback, which Amazon supports, the back cover becomes important. Your book would sometimes be placed on the backside and the readers might not see the illustration in front.

The back cover could contain your blurb, which will help arouse your prospective reader's curiosity.

Also, it is a good place to show off your name. As a new writer, your title should be bigger than your name at the front cover. In the back cover, however, the two could have the same size.

Creating Your Cover on a Budget

Professional Kindle cover makers charge about $30 for a cover and you do not even get the copyright for it. Some other writers can use the same cover for their book. If you want to have the copyright, the maker could charge you for over $100. That would be a big amount for an aspiring novelist.

Thus, it is better to create your own cover. Here are some ways to come up with a cover in a budget.

1. ***Ask your friends to be your model.*** The reason original copyrighted covers are expensive is because of the model. The owner of the picture should also have a release from the model and that means extra payment.

Instead of using professional models, ask help from some of your friends, who fit the description of your character. Your friends might do it for free.

Your other friends can also help with your models' wardrobe and makeup.

2. _Look for free images in the internet._ There are many sites that allow other people to upload their pictures on the net. Some of them allow the public to use their images for free. However, you should be careful in choosing pictures with models. Some of these models may not have signed a release form to the uploader. The picture may be used for social media, but may not be used for profit.

3. _Take your own pictures._ Smartphones now have features that allow you to take pictures like a professional. You can use it to take your own pictures that depict the story you want to convey.

For example, if you are writing about a love story that started or ended with a wedding banquet, you can simply get pictures of a wedding banquet and incorporate it with your models or use it as it is.

It is free and you also get the copyright for it. You might earn from that picture and your novel.

4. _Draw your own cover._ Some books have caricatures or anime drawings for a cover. Some are pastel drawings or simple artworks. If you have a talent in drawing or painting, you can draw your own cover.

After you have drawn it, scan it and edit it to fit your cover. Again, it is free and you get the copyright.

5. _Learn the basics of Photoshop._ Hiring graphic artists will also cost you a lot, even when they only use the basics of Photoshop. You can make good covers by just understanding the basics of Photoshop. Here are some tools and commands that you have to understand because you will be using them a lot:

a. *Quick select tool.* This is helpful when you are trying to remove the background and complicated shapes of the picture. You can also use it when you want to copy or edit only a portion of the image.

b. *Erase tool.* This is often use in layering, especially when you want to use the outline of the previous layer and remove the current outline of the image. It is helpful when creating mirror or reflexive effects.

c. *Adding and removing the layer.* Layering allows you to add another slide over the first one you created. It allows you to add other items on the previous slide, but does not change the original slide. Thus, when you erase or remove the top layer, the previous slides would still be preserved. You do not have to scrap the whole thing when you make a mistake in a certain layer.

d. *Screen command.* This is a layering command which allows you to filter some properties of the image and leave you with a lighter image with fading outlines. It is good for creating smoky effects.

e. *Lighting, Darkening and Dissolve.* These are also layering commands that help you to adjust the color of your image.

f. *Blending and filtering commands.* Blending effects are intermediate commands, but learning a few of them can make your cover more attractive.

g. *Transforming commands.* Flipping and rotating your picture can help you layout your cover better. But, one thing you should really consider mastering is the **freeform transforming.** This command could help you place objects in your image without the need of reshooting.

For example, if you want to place sunglasses to your model, you can just place separate sunglasses and transform it until it fits your model's face. The freeform command is very useful. You should try to explore it a lot.

6. *Learn the basics of PowerPoint Text and Wordart commands.* The text command in Photoshop is a little complicated for beginners. The Powerpoint Wordart is easier. You can edit your titles and your name using these commands. Save them as an image and add it to your layer in Photoshop.

You may also save the image in Photoshop and add your title and your name using the Powerpoint Text commands.

7. *Use the Kindle Cover maker.* Kindle Direct Publishing, which we will cover in the next chapter, offers tools to their writers. One of the tools is the cover maker. They offer free images, which you can use and offer ready-made styles for your white spaces, titles and name. The application is fairly easy to use, but it is limited.

To make the most out of the application, it would be better to use your own image for the cover and use the feature that allows you to add the title and your name.

Chapter Eight:
Setting Up Your Amazon Kindle Direct Publishing Account

The famous and easiest way to individually publish your novel or books is through the Amazon Kindle Direct Publishing. It offers many tools and applications that will help you publish your book. All you need is a manuscript that fits their page layout and technical requirement.

It also offers promotion and advertising methods to help you introduce and sell your books to the rest of the world. In this chapter, you will be presented with a thorough walk through on how to set up your Kindle Direct Publishing (KDP) account, how to publish your book, and how to sell and promote it.

A. Setting Your KDP Account

Step 1: Getting an Amazon account.

You need to have a valid Amazon account to register in Amazon KDP. Setting up an Amazon account is simple. You only need to have a valid e-mail address. Your profile in your Amazon account can be different from your profile in Amazon KDP. Visit **https://www.amazon.com/**, to set up an account if you haven't already.

Step 2: Going to kdp.amazon.com

If you cannot get to the site directly, just type "kindle direct publishing amazon" and you will find it in the search results page.

You will be asked for your Amazon account. Here, you can use your Amazon account's password to enter or you can enter in as a new user.

Once you get inside, you will be asked to fill up your profile.

Step 3: Setting up your KDP profile

On the first page of your profile, you will have to enter your author or publisher information, tax information, and bank account. You do not have to complete all of them at once. You could concentrate on the author or publisher information first. You could fill up the rest after you have decided to publish your book.

You need to complete all the information before you could withdraw the sales for your books.

Step 4: Hit "Save"

Save your information and you are ready to start publishing through kindle.

B. Publishing Your Book

At the top portion of the KDP page, you will find the tab for "bookshelf". That is where you will start to publish your work. Here are the steps:

Step 1: Go to the space that says "Create your title".

There would be two buttons available. One is for kindle books and the other is for paperback. To start publishing your kindle books, choose the kindle books.

Step 2: Fill up the eBook details.

In this section, you will be asked for the language of your novel, the title or subtitle. You can skip the spaces for the "series" and "edition" if you are publishing your novel for the first time.

You have to fill the author's name. You need to let the people know who you are. However, you may not enter your real name. You can enter your pen name instead. As for the space in the contributors, you can enter the name of your editor or co-authors to credit them, if any.

Step 3: Give a professional description.

In the eBook details, there is a space for the description of your book. It is the description that will appear in the page of your book in Amazon.com. It gives the readers and prospective buyers a glimpse of what your novel is about.

Since it is only limited to 4000 characters, you have to make it short, straight and effective. But, this is where you will grab the majority of customers so make it stand out!

Step 4: Declare your copyright ownership.

In the same page, you will be asked if you own the copyright of your novel or if it is a public domain. You should declare that you own the copyright. If the book is of public domain, you may be required to present additional information that permits you to publish it.

Step 5: Choose your keywords.

Keywords are tags for your novels. You will be allowed up to 7 keywords. Make sure that you write good keywords. Some of your keywords could be the genre of your novel, the nature of your characters. Limit your keywords to 1-3 words per space. The longer your keywords are, the lesser hits it may get. Don't include your Title or Name as theses will already show up in a search.

Step 6: Choose your Categories.

The KDP allows you to choose only 2 categories. Some of the categories have its sub-categories. Unlike the keywords, make your categories specific. You should narrow the category, so your book could be lined up easily in the ranking.

Step 7: Fill or skip the age and grade space.

You could fill this space if you want, but Amazon sometimes corrects it for you. So, it would be better to just skip it.

Step 8: Choose when to publish your book.

There are two choices in this section. You can either publish your book right away or set it up for a pre-order. As a new writer, it would be better to publish your book right away. Setting your book for a pre-order may trigger other writer to copy your idea and publish their work earlier than yours.

Step 9: Save your details and continue to Kindle eBook content.

You can also choose to save it as a draft if your eBook content is not ready.

Step 10: Read the content guidelines and know the supported files.

The pages of your eBook would be similar to how you formatted your manuscript. If your format is a mess, your e-book will also be a mess. Read the content guidelines first before uploading your manuscript to make your eBook look neat and professional.

The KDP only supports a few files. Manuscripts saved as Microsoft Word documents usually do not create any problem when it is uploaded.

Step 11: Choose your Digital Right Management (DRM) option.

If you enroll your novel in DRM, the readers could not share it with other kindle readers. It is a good way to increase your sales. However, if you want to establish your name as an author, publishing some of your novels outside the DRM can help.

Step 12: Upload your Manuscript

Press the "upload manuscript" tab. A window will open, allowing you to choose the manuscript you want to publish. Wait until it is uploaded successfully. The application will also inform you if there are some possible grammatical or spelling errors in your manuscript, so you could correct and re-upload it.

Step 13: Upload your Cover

KDP gives you two options. You can make your cover using their cover creator app, as discussed in Chapter 7 or upload your own image. Only TIFF and JPG files are allowed. Make sure that your image is more than 300kb, so it will not look pixelated.

Step 14: Preview your eBook

You can skip this step, but it is recommended. Here, you can see how your book will look like in a kindle reader. Just launch the previewer to preview your book.

Step 15: Skip the last section or fill it.

The last portion about the ISBN or publisher is not necessary. Amazon would provide for the ISBN and the publisher can always be left blank.

Step 16: Hit "Save and Continue" to set up your book pricing.

You have to save the contents, so it will be completely uploaded. You may also save it as a draft if you are not ready to publish it

C. <u>Pricing and Selling Your Book</u>
Step 1: Decide whether to enroll in KDP select or not

KDP select is a contract of exclusivity with Amazon. If you enroll your novel, you must not publish the digital copy of your novel in other sites that offer individual publishing like Goodreads.

When you enroll in KDP select however, you may be entitled to bigger royalties.

Step 2: Select the territories where you want to publish your novel.

If you want worldwide success, just tick the worldwide option. If you only want to sell your book in specific territories, then choose it from the list.

Step 3: Select the Royalty and Pricing for your book.

Royalty is the amount you will receive when your book is purchased. KDP offers 35% and 70% royalty options.

However, the 70% royalty options have some conditions. To qualify for this option, you should enroll in KDP select and your book should not be lower than $2.99.

Step 4: Enroll or skip the other ride-on options, like matchbook and book lending.

Matchbook is allowing the people, who bought a paperback copy of your novel, to buy the kindle copy at a discount.

Book lending is allowing other reader to lend the copies of their books with other readers.

Step 5: Read the terms and conditions.

You can skip this step, but it is highly recommended that you read it. You will understand more about pricing and receiving your sales through it.

If you agree to it, publish your book by clicking on the "publish your kindle eBook" button.

Step 6: Promote your book

After you have published your book, you will be directed to a bookshelf. Here, you can see all the books you saved as drafts or books you had publish.

In the table of the details, you will see column for kindle eBook actions. Drop the arrow and choose promote and advertise. However, you have to be enrolled in KDP select to be eligible for the promotion.

You will be presented with two options:

1. **The free book promotion.** You will be offering your book for free at a certain period. It is a good way to get some readers to read your novel and gain some reviews. Reviews can help the popularity of your book. You are only eligible for a free promotion for 5 days, every 90 days. You can use them as and when you desire but I would recommend using all 5 consecutively in order to attract more audience.

2. **The countdown deal.** The price of your book will be increased in a staggered manner. You will start with a cheaper and discounted price and end it with the regular price you set. This is only available for books priced at $2.99 or more.

Chapter Nine:
Creating a Professional Description and Blurb

Your book description and blurbs give your reader a good glimpse of what your story is about. It is often found at the back of the paperback or in the page for the digital copy. It is both an advertising tool and a creative tool for promoting your books.

The reader might buy your book because of the description. They may become interested with the story because of them, too. A description and/or blurb are crucial to the success of your novel in the market. Thus, you should create them in a professional and creative way.

Below are some points to consider when creating your description and blurb:

1. Make your description or your blurb tell your idea in an exciting way.

Excite your possible readers with your description or blurb. It is like pitching. You are setting you novel apart from other novels with the similar plot. If your novel is romantic, write a description that would make your reader become excited to fall in love. If you write a thriller, excite your reader about discovering the secrets.

Excited readers will most likely buy your novel. So, make sure to elicit feeling from them when you are writing your description or blurb.

2. *Be particular with the first line.* Many readers get hooked to the novel by the first line in the description, the blurb or the first chapter. The first line sets the tone of your novel.

There are a few ways of doing it. You can start it with a strong dialogue from your novel. This could arouse the curiosity of your reader.

For example: "You are guilty!" Leo's world was about to crumble because of those three words.

You can also use a question to your reader and use the rest to tell them about how they could find the answer in your story.

You may also use quotes that could give your reader a clue on what your novel is about.

3. *Tell a short summary of your novel up to the conflicting part.* This is only applicable for the description and not the blurb. If you keep your reader hanging, they might be intrigued enough to buy your book.

4. *Make a reference to a best seller.* This is usually frowned upon by critical readers, but it attracts most readers. You can write that your story can get the reader excited about remembering the feeling when they were reading the certain best-seller. However, always point out that your novel puts a twist on the plot of the best-seller.

For example: Relieve a modern story based on "Romeo and Juliet", but will take you into a roller coaster ride of teenage romance filled with comedy and tragedy.

5. ***Try talking about your characters and the conflicts they have to resolve.*** A good character can be used in your description. You can describe him and his character and present the challenge he needed to resolve.

For example: Leo is a veteran FBI agent who solved dozens of cold cases because of his persistence. But, when his son was found dead in a dumpster, Leo could not trace who the killer is. Will his persistence triumph over the murderer, who seems to know how to evade justice? Or will his son's case become the cold case he could never solve?

6. *Do not talk or promote yourself.* In your first novel, avoid putting your qualifications in your description. Some writers do that because they think that readers would want to read books written by intelligent or award-winning people. The description should be about your story and not who you are.

So, avoid writing lines like, "The writer is a former crime scene investigator and he wrote the story exactly how it could happen." This might not help attract readers to your novel.

Conclusion

Thank you for buying *How to Write a Best-Selling Book in 30 Days: An Easy-to-Follow Guide on How To Create, Write and Publish Your Own Book.*

I hope that this book encouraged you to continue achieving your dream to become a novelist. As you have read, there are now ways to publish your books on your own. You do not need to impress any publisher just to start your career as a writer.

Your only enemy now is yourself. So, I suggest that you collect that willpower, courage and confidence to write your novels. There are many ideas surrounding you and many resources you can now use to complete your novel. Do not let yourself hinder your own success.

Thank you again for reading this book. I hope to be reading your novel soon!

Be sure to leave a review on Amazon for me, and feel free to let me know of any new novelists out there!

It's been a pleasure.

Good luck on this new adventure, I sincerely hope it's your best one yet.

DW.

63944350R00034

Made in the USA
Lexington, KY
23 May 2017